abdobooks.com

Published by Abdo Zoom, a division of ABDO, P.O. Box 398166, Minneapolis, Minnesota 55439. Copyright © 2024 by Abdo Consulting Group, Inc. International copyrights reserved in all countries. No part of this book may be reproduced in any form without written permission from the publisher. Fly!™ is a trademark and logo of Abdo Zoom.

Printed in the United States of America, North Mankato, Minnesota.
052023
092023

THIS BOOK CONTAINS RECYCLED MATERIALS

Photo Credits: Alamy, AP Images, Getty Images, Shutterstock, US Navy
Production Contributors: Kenny Abdo, Jennie Forsberg, Grace Hansen
Design Contributors: Candice Keimig, Neil Klinepier, Laura Graphenteen

Library of Congress Control Number: 2022946928

Publisher's Cataloging-in-Publication Data

Names: Abdo, Kenny, author.
Title: Adventure records to get your heart racing! / by Kenny Abdo
Description: Minneapolis, Minnesota : Abdo Zoom, 2024 | Series: Broken records | Includes online resources and index.
Identifiers: ISBN 9781098281366 (lib. bdg.) | ISBN 9781098282066 (ebook) | ISBN 9781098282417 (Read-to-me ebook)
Subjects: LCSH: Records--Juvenile literature. | History--Juvenile literature. | Adventure and adventurers--Juvenile literature.
Classification: DDC 032.02--dc23

TABLE OF CONTENTS

Adventure Records 4

Broken Records 8

For the Record 20

Glossary 22

Online Resources 23

Index 24

Adventure Records

Throughout history, people have looked for adventure. And by pushing themselves, humans have achieved world records along the way!

From long distance drives to **freefalling** from the Earth's **stratosphere**, these records will get anyone's heart racing!

BROKEN RECORDS

In 1888, Bertha Benz told her husband that she was going on a road trip. The drive was 66 miles (106 km) long. That made Benz the first person to drive an automobile over a long distance!

While in the **Royal Navy**, Poon Lim's ship was attacked in 1942. He survived 133 days alone at sea. Lim was picked up by a fishing boat in 1943. He earned the record for longest time spent surviving at sea on a life raft.

In 2012, Felix Baumgartner did a **freefall** jump from 24 miles (39 km) above Earth's surface. He attained the record for highest manned balloon flight, the fastest speed in freefall, and first human to break the **sound barrier**!

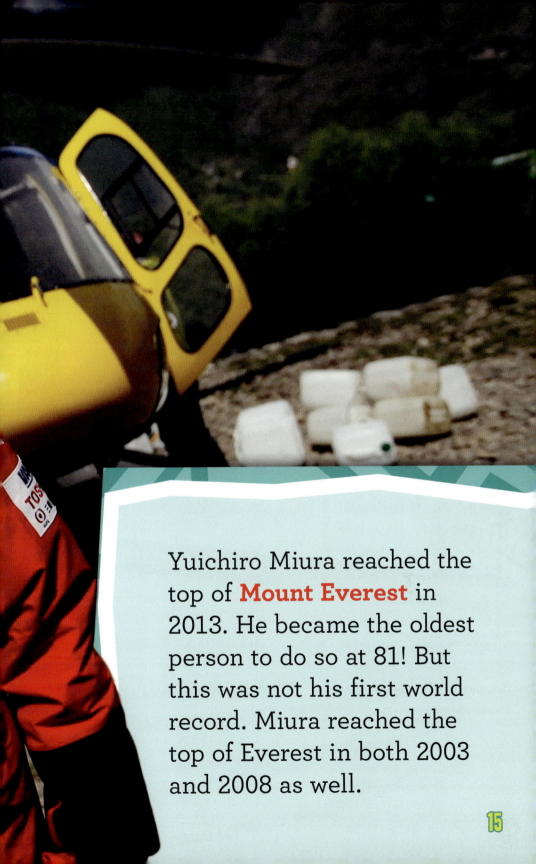

Yuichiro Miura reached the top of **Mount Everest** in 2013. He became the oldest person to do so at 81! But this was not his first world record. Miura reached the top of Everest in both 2003 and 2008 as well.

In 2018, Denise Mueller-Korenek wanted to see how fast bikes could really go. She rode a specialty bike hitched to a **dragster**. Mueller-Korenek set a new bike speed record of 183.9 mph (296 kmh), smashing the previous record of 167 mph (269 kmh)!

Surfer Sebastian Steudtner rode a 115-foot (35 m) wave in 2022. He surpassed the previous world record that he set himself, receiving a new **Guinness World Record** for the highest wave ever surfed!

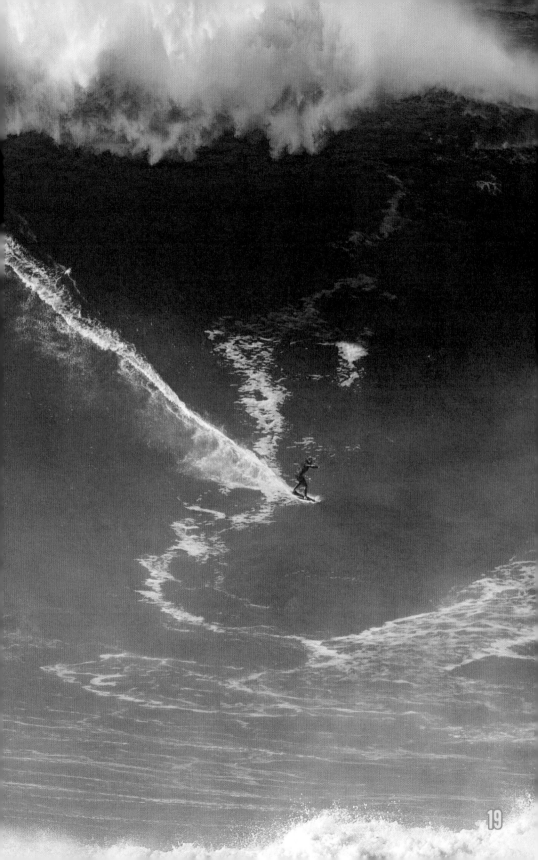

FOR THE RECORD

For most adventurers, the journey matters more than the destination. But sometimes the journey ends with a world record!

GLOSSARY

dragster – a modified car built to perform in drag races.

freefall – the portion of skydiving when the parachute is not used.

Guinness World Record – an award given to those who have broken a record never achieved before.

Mount Everest – Earth's highest mountain that is above sea level. It is part of the Himalayan mountains, along the China and Nepal border.

Royal Navy – the United Kingdom's sea warfare force.

sound barrier – a sudden large increase in aerodynamic drag that occurs as the speed of an aircraft approaches the speed of sound.

stratosphere – a layer of the Earth's upper atmosphere from about six miles to about thirty miles above the earth's surface.

ONLINE RESOURCES

To learn more about adventure records, please visit **abdobooklinks.com** or scan this QR code. These links are routinely monitored and updated to provide the most current information available.

INDEX

Baumgartner, Felix 13

Benz, Bertha 8

distance 8

Guinness World Record (award) 18

Lim, Poon 11

Miura, Yūichirō 15

Mount Everest 15

Mueller-Korenek, Denise 16

speed 13, 16

Steudtner, Sebastian 18

surfing 18